THE ROSE OF KABUL

A COLLECTION OF POETRY IN TOUCH OF PERSIAN

ROYA WAHAB

Copyright © Roya Wahab
All Rights Reserved.

This book has been published with all efforts taken to make the material error-free after the consent of the author. However, the author and the publisher do not assume and hereby disclaim any liability to any party for any loss, damage, or disruption caused by errors or omissions, whether such errors or omissions result from negligence, accident, or any other cause.

While every effort has been made to avoid any mistake or omission, this publication is being sold on the condition and understanding that neither the author nor the publishers or printers would be liable in any manner to any person by reason of any mistake or omission in this publication or for any action taken or omitted to be taken or advice rendered or accepted on the basis of this work. For any defect in printing or binding the publishers will be liable only to replace the defective copy by another copy of this work then available.

Contents

Acknowledgements

I want to like to thanks to all my family members and my Freinds who support me in this journey.

It is my heartfelt thank to all of you who helped in these Journey,

1. Childhood

Childhood

"Birth

In the valley of Love a Tulip Grows ;

The silent haze of wool crawled in her tiny hands.
She had generosity that peaks in the vast Mountains,
In the mid of July, the season of summer burs leaves;
Life is summoned in the vivid wall of mysterious birth.
Oh! Moon do you hear the resonance of her tiny feet,
She was the Piece of the red angel which was created in light of beauty.
Oh! Moon do you resemble the smile of her in the dusk of wind,
She fainted in the loop of curvature to the sigh of love.
In the jar of full of Hopes, The thread of magic rolled ;
On her arrival, No one understands the thickness of the thread
That rolled in her arms to shine in the vivid light of the sky.
"1998"

Eyes inquired in tales of a grueling journey of destiny
"Why did the sand touch her feet?" in a dim voice
The new Phase of life is sculpted an ounce of voice
Fade the memory of old Pictures in dim Phase of destiny ;
One tinted canvas of old Picture adorned in her voice,
To the valley of tulips that grow in the hills of Kabul.
Almighty! My heart is deranged in love with you
This world told me" I am Insane Lover" with a Pinch of salt
I collected the bouquet and adorn it on myself
They said " Look, the Insane Lover wanna be beautiful"
I collected the dirt and adore it in my hands with salt

They said " Look, the Insane Lover is ugly " while giggling.
I replied " Tho, flower to the sand adorn the creation of the lord"
A flower never blooms without mud, my lord created the piece of mud
That I want to erode on myself for the love of you ;
Almighty! My heart is alluring in the shadow of faith.

"Sunflower"

Waving the edge of memorizing my heart tangled in the Garden
I still recall the trees, flowers, fruits, and the sweet smell of the Garden
There is not the fantasy but the view of my house was in the Kabul

The sunflower was one of the flowers that bloom in the garden of my motherland
My Motherland sounds like the sweet gesture of " Land of love".
Oh! Who you stash in the window of haze moist of cloud;
The Garden of love is filled with the roses of different colors of my Motherland.
Waving the side of memorizing my heart tangled in the Gardner
I still recall sunflowers that bloomed on the surface of the mud
This is not a fantasy but the view of my house was in the Kabul
Lapsed cold wind shatter the door of life in the breeze of that scenario
Sunflowers grow in the valley of the blood of innocent martyrs in my motherland!
Birds chatter and nested the house for their shielder while wind dusk it in the sand;
Waving the side of memories my heart tangled in the Garden of Sunflowers!

"Beauty"

Frightened in a vision of the imaginary the lord blessed her
The beauty which swaddles and calm the soul of belovers
In the midnight lamp burn the light of her, roads rides
To the sight of the beholder the merchants were die in that beauty;
Hurry! In the walk of meadow grass, a sign simulated her,
Lommy's enchanted eyes of the stranger fell in the beauty of her.
Frightened in a vision of the imaginary our lord blessed her
The beauty which swaddles and calm the soul of belovers
She was the most beautiful child that born in the valley of love
The blush of her cheek glorify the Purity of her heart
Twirl shadow of her beauty whirl the story of the Rose
That blossom in the red soft lips in the moist of her heart
Frightened in the vision of the imaginary our lord blessed her
The beauty which swaddles and calm the soul of belovers
Do you hear the voice of beauty beneath the love of an ounce?
World transgresses and metaphors to knit the story of that Beauty.

" Farsi" (Persian)

What should I Pray to Allah for? whose words are in the language of love

What should I want the Almighty for? Whose Speaks the tune of love

Oh! Who you read this, My words are not mine but the fragment of Farsi

The day and night resemble the shadow of love in the words of Farsi

My heart is incapable of love of the tulips that stuck in the words of Farsi

What should I pray to Allah for? Whose words are in the language of love

What should I want the Almighty for? Whose Speaks the tune of love

My lord did miracle to chatter the words of truth in the tune of love

Oh! The creator of the world let entangled my words in the sigh of love

To the shaded old Pictures of thread
It bouquet the mien of remembrance
A Pretty face in the old Picture of threat
with Tiny hands in the cartilage of the room
Has collapsed in the mien of remembrance
Time, cuddle the old memory of love
Every time, Eyes meet in the visage
It blossom happiness; Heart meet
And burnt in the flames of love.

"Her Visage"

Her visage is still in the window of my heart,
Her innocence is still a glimmer in her eyes,
The dreams melted in the corner of her eyes,
Her visage is still in the window of my heart,
Do you hear the calm soothing voice of life?
Her Purity of heart is scattering in the glam of her heart!
From flowers to the soft touch of wind and each doorstep
It gather the desire of humanity, She was the true
Meaning of kindness, The thorns touched her and wounded her.
Still, she sang the song of the Peace in broken self.
Her Visage is still in the moist drops of time,
How could someone be that gentle? My heart
Rushed to touch the innocence of her!
The soft touch of her still lives inside me!

"The Rose of Kabul"

A rose grew in the hill of Kabul
That Pluck the story of love in her small hands
Oh! Caretaker of the rose, Let melted the water
Into steam to Pacify each drizzle of the Kabul
Into the layers of the love in the mount of the Rose
And the love of wounds that makes her charm!
Let Pleated the story of love in that charm
Oh! caretaker of the rose, let care of her hands
Her destiny melted with the life of petals!
The glow on the face of the rose and blush
foregather in ropes of it, it melted the beauty of petals.

'Smile'

Last Night I saw the dream
In which I wrote the Poetry on "smile"
It was the Mid Night that necromancer
My heart to the Pleasing journey of life
The time reside the Phenomena of the life
We abhor adorning the Pleasing sign on it.
Last Night I saw the dream
In which I wrote the Poetry on "smile"
It decode my heart to the memories of Childhood
The small girl with long brown golden hair and red lips
And Hush the stain blush on her cheeks , the Brooke
The smile was coat in her face like a magnet in Iron.
As the time rushes, the smile has stin in vask
Of flowers that bloom far in the valley.

Hash! The troubles and crumbles.
She was afraid of the shore of wind
She had the voice that soothes the hate,
Hash! The troubles and the sign,
Her softness pick in the shyness of her,
My lord, take care the soft voice of her,
Hash! The troubles and crumbles.
She was afraid of the shore of wind
Do you hear the sign of her voice?
The small footprints of her , Rush the
Troubles , the first flight of migration
To the land of the foreigners in Shore
Her voice glazed the Pain in young age!

" Sky"

In the open surface of the lamp
The fire burn to tranquilize the
Momentum of the clouds ;
It moves with the heavy heart
To shape on the curvature of the
Sight , No one Place them in
The shape of them , Here the
Sky devastated and tears to fall
In the land in the form of water;
Each trops of the tears had shaped
The thirst of the land in the soothing
Sight of the sky , The fire meet
The glance of sky as child mould
Themselves to thought morals of
Life , it gleaned and Tears.

" Story Book"
Turning the Pages of the colorful stories
To ! cork the sound of the chattering Nightingale,
I scummed in the middle page of hope,
The stories give me the relief of life ;
Fox, Owl, Lion & the Birds are the mirages of it,
The stories Pleated the New hope of Adventure.
Stories Book stir the heart in the journey of it.
Turning the Pages of the Colorful Stories
To the story of Prince and the owls
Each moment gives the aroma of Heaven.

"Widows"

Looking down in the tearing face of widows,
My heart always looked in the Pain of her,
The story is tangled and the sad,
They were the Widows of Afghanistan,
The land has a history of pain and beauty,
I want to kiss their Pain and scars from the head
To the tie , The blood run from her eyes ,
Don't cry my loves the blood pleated into the eyes,
Her story calm the Pain of the Mud,
The Windows of Afghanistan lives in my heart!

For Child , to Understand the story is
Intensify the pain and reality of the life,
The ting drops of tears on her eyes
Burns the blue sky and blaze the soil
God! Never torture their creature like that
I wish , Once should I ask to God
About her destiny to make it wicked!

In Window of Imagination, the life sculpted on it,
Charming Prince come in the top of the grass in it,
Hurry, Rushed in the castle of the Imagination ;
Long Purple gown downfall in the ground,
With the open long golden hair in it ;
In Window of Imagination, the life sculpted in it
The horse is running in the valley of the garden!
Princess should run with her long hair
And fall in the arms of Prince , The stories
Augment the pond of imagination and joy.
In Window of Imagination, the life sculpted on it,
Charming Prince come in the top of the grass in it
Might , the love comes with the first moves of the
Heart in horse with Prince or it will become nightmare
The vast window of imagination is ruined with the flowers of
it.

" Fairy Tales"

Fairy tales have beautiful boundary of Fasicanation
It steal the lover with beauty of love , the story
Wrote in the vivid candles to burn the flames of Fasication
I wrote it in the day to the stars of the Night
That drawn me the the story of the Happiness
The life born and die To pull the Barrier of love.

.

It was the joyful journey of the life

It give the sensation of immense love.

" Immigration"

Oh! The Gaspy when you travelled

Did you hear the crushing sound of wind?
That leave in the footprint when you leave the Place ;
Oh! The Gaspy when you last time
Leave your homeland, do your feet stuck on it?
I migrated on my homeland at age of five
It gives me the Painful retrivation of the life
The land was dusted and painted in the tiny hopes of life
I cultivated in the love of that phase which will never be mine!

"My dearest friend"
My dearest friend you had the most pretty face,
The time spent with you is like the jewels,
I loved the way you were be with me,
No one here is like her ; so, I kept
Her visage at the bottom of my heart!
My Dearest Friend you had the most Pretty Face,
The smile of you is still in the grass of Paintings
That I kept in my heart , Times runs like water ,
You have the love of heaven and the voice of water
That was drunk by the passenger to keep drunk in the stories.
No , One is here was like her ; So , I kept her in the bottom
In my heart , life is Red and you make it Blue !

"The Time we shared"

The Time we shared was hooked in memory of my cage
The old house and the bouquet of the smile on your face
The dollhouse and the toys with whom we Played ;
Time entangled the rhythm of us, the thread separate us;
Into the two Pieces but the memory shattered in my head ;
I love the way we make the dollhouse, You imprison my
Heart in dwell memory of You, I want to catch you someday
In that old house to Playing with doll house and the bouquet
With a smile on your face , That time entangles us and
separates us.

When I was nine years I read the complete Quran;
Allah bestows his favor to me, I cartilage the words
Of sacred book in my mouth, Bismillah is chatter
In my mouth since morning to Night, I was the
Believer of my lord with the Purest heart ;
My love to Islam dwell like stars in my heart ;
It was the most precious book , Which I was
Read ; If you fell in love with the love , then
It's wording tell you the truth of the life ;
I am abhor to the Night when someone wants
That I detached to these beautiful scriptures
It will turn myself into ashes and nothing left
Except the wording of Quran dance in the Fire!

"Books"
Oh my dear love! How could I forget you ?
It's known other than books than drawn

In the depth of my heart to circulate in my blood
The life is born and the true friend were found in it;
I blaze it in the blanket of the hope , to fall the rain
Of knowledge on my eyes as each time I lift my eyelashes
So , I saw the true Friend in the wording of books.

2. Younger

Younger

The footstep"

The footstep was smuggled in the roa"d of Mud ;

The free Bird is taken the first flight of journey ;
In the Open dream of sky , the eagle took first flight;
Hurry rush is smuggled in the roads of Hopes;
No , one could be emphasis in the jar of hope ;
There is rush in the road that smuggled in it ;
The footstep is smuggled in the Road of Mud;

"Friends"

The journey in the bond of friends ,
Two unveiling long road crossed together;
Oh! Yeah, we laughed together in those days;
The days chatter in the arms of laughter;
Pain, agony was holding together with friends;
The quiet tales of story sung the saga of life
The room, voices, and the times changed in the life
The journey excluded in the bond of friends
Oh! Yeah, we laughed together in those days,

" Peacock"

Peacock has breath the first sign of love ;
The breath Suddenly Become Slow;

It was the sign of the first flight she gleaned;
She was afraid of the harsh words of Birds;
Her Heart cunning in the vicious tale ;
Her calmness is Peak in the gesture;
The Breath Suddenly become slow;
Her beauty has sparkled in the colors of her
But Pain gathers in the steps of her;

" Sensitivity"

Her Sensitivity Peak in the gesture of her ;
The world is too tough for her soft heart;
She Afraid of the cruel words of the world ;
She was soft like the Petals of Rose, That falls intensely ;
My Heart still Sung the beauty of the girl ;
Her Sensitivity Peak in the gesture of her;
The cartilage of together bouquet is tie together ;
Like her Beauty, The life Sung the Song of her beauty

Tears wear fall from the heaven
When the heart Moist the song of love

It is the Journey of the love that Peak
It would be the song of the Place,
Rain is cartilage in the Beauty of the Song,
No one Heard So, I sing that song
The tear is in the voice of the believer
That tune in the Purity of heart
It falls from heaven to the
Sign of love, that is shown by love.

Rain Down in the surface of the sky
To shine that gloomy cloud on it
Do you hear the sound of thunder?
The crystal light of the Rainbow
My heart Sparkled in the gloomy voice of it
The sound of thunder that fall in moist
It brings the sun to the surface of it
Raindrops bloomed in the echoes of the voice
My heart fell in the loving gesture of it

My mother told me “ Don’t pull yourself down for Men”
When you love him then don’t forget your respect ;
My mother told me “ Don’t be the women that own by men”
When you have your self-respect to shine in the sky
My mother told me” Don’t share your deep sacres with him”
When he is angered then he doesn’t respect it
My mother told me “ Never be the women that afraid to the crowd”
When you are born as a strong human to be a woman.

Tear drops don't crystal down in your lips
The soft sound be the first Flight to be strong
No worry Mealt, My heart anymore
I told the game changer to be the worst Human
I was born to be the ruler of this world
This is just the sign of My Imagination
Tears encapsulated in the enchanter sound of the cage

That was born to be bloomed in the stars of the sky
The soft sound bloomed as the flayer voice of love

Karachi Bomb Blast

" It will be the tragic story that wiped in the sky
The old man whipped the tears of blood from his heart
My heart shattered in the pieces, To catch the aroma of it
The tears fall from his eyes,
The eyes were Moist and the hands are shivering
In his situation, the sky has a thunderstorm
It will be the tragic story that wiped in the sky
My heart shattered into a the Pisces to catch the
From of it in the " Karachi Bomb Blast"

New Magic arrived in the touch of adolescence
The friends, Chattering gossips, Rumours have made the flowers

It gives the first wing to the eagle to fly
The Rose pleated the petals of love in it ;
New Magic arrived in the touch of Adolescence,
No one Heard this, But wrote it in the song of it

The sadness tackled the surrounding of it ;
Oh! Who lived in the voice of the shadow,
Now Tackled the sound of love on it,
The sadness tackled & encapsulated or Broke the window of happiness.

Books Have the comfort that bounded the love
This comfort gives Life has the joy of love and the
Pain has the love of partner;
Books have the comfort that encapsulated in the sky;
His Comfort give the joy of love to the lover;

Science

It will the New World to me the Technology ;
The clouds have the candy of perception on it ;
The life is unpredictable the truth is the light
While carbon is the dirt of the wind ;
It will be the theories that surrender by heart ;
The Science have the New World to me the technology ;
The clouds have the candy of perception on ti

Adulthood has the adventure of the town ;
A dull face bloomed again in the happiness

The torn have the fantasy of the road
Some nights are the Silence , Where is the love of life
No one Hear the sound of it ;
It can bloom in the dark days to the diary Nights
Adulthood teach me the sign of love ;
No one Hear it, So it Falls on it

Some Nights are too Heavy for Sleep
No one can listen to the Rhythm of your soul
I can bloom it in My way for it ;
Do you hear the voice of love in it ;
The silent voice the viscous touch gives the Glimmer of it ;
My Heart Ruin to Catch the beauty of it ;
Do you hear the Negation of it?

A drop of rain falls on my hands
It drenched out the life on my sigh
I felt balminess in each drop
There was something
Which attract me to the beauty
Of life and desire of mine.

It would Anomalous the wind touch you,
On Grief that touch riddim saga of love
And as the hands move to hold the touch
Isn't Anomalous that sigh flattered in Haze
That turning in Pieces of the breath
Well we couldn't touch nor see the haze
But yet it riddim in the touch of that wind
Isn't Anomalous hows the words Pleaded
To tore and frame the magic of love

I still remember that girl
Whose words blossom the flowers
Her Politeness water the thirsty buds
I still remember that girl
Whose shyness Manifest in her smile
Like a riddim light in night of haze
I still remember that girl
Whose gesture Pearl the wind of heaven
In the gloominess of voices calm the shores
I still remember that girl
Who didn't drift the bitterness in her tongue
I still remember that girl
Who lost in ages in the beauty of her heart

My heart quiver in the loamy soil of blood ;
Nobody could hear its beat in-crowd the;
So, Lemme sleep in a sweet dream of
The peace that escaped my Pain in the dust!
Nights crawled in the beauty of illusion
And my eyes filled in the blood of tears,
When the sunrises my hands wiped
The blood and manifest life in a Gardner of illusion

Would the sorrow shrink in the garden
Of heavenliness, more delicate than glass?
Yet the sounds reiterate in majesty ,
Of dwell wasteland of the gardner ;
That sing holy words of pain in majesty,
To bloom the story of life in the garden .
To hearken the seed of happiness
In relief of the " the Sacrifice!"

3. Essence of Love

Essence of Love

Lipton the arms of my sigh in the stranger
It whirled the doms of love in the goblet
Of the imagination of the who sews the
Arch of the love in the Pool of water
Tho, I sewed the one Place of my Heart
For the smile of the stranger , it melt
My reflection in the merge of him
Lipton the arms of my sign in the stranger
The vision of the love seemed to be sweeten
That taste of words in the the Goblet of the love
I have to winged in the sigh of him, it calmed the
Love of my sign in the voice of you who listen!

"Holy sin"

The rhythm of you is sculpture me into a piece
Where I melting my sorrow's in a melody of love
Someday's this searing affection scared me,
And plucking intoxicating waves from the veins.
That merging a cup of wine in my blood
They say it is a holy sin ,which I drunk every night
Till the light sparkles and dusted into dark
Where my heart stand like a cloud in a gloomy drama
The phases is aparted but the theme is remain in you,
In the viscous sea my life is drown in the breeze
Of a cold waves which diverged in the arc of love
At the moment breeze touches the mud
And my feeling sparkled and mounted underneath the water
I found it pocius as the verse of the holy book
In which my heart rytm in the saga of love
Still they say it's a holy sin
Some nights the thoughts of the sin is merged me,
While some days I kept chatter the melody of that love
Sin is seems to pandering that I kept melt my body

For one touch of your love and dim into light of hell
The arabic verses collapsing a bond of mumming sound
In which every night a believer closed the eyes
In a dream of love it's fansating
How's love would be sin when you and me are the creator one
Yet they say it's a holy sin ,it's a holy sin
If it's a holy sin let buried myself in a cage
And I want to fly in the rhythm of that love

My words died in the saga of your charming face ;
I wished I would die in the vivid dream of your love .
This feelings makes my heart incongruous in your love ;
I am nothing than than the Yousuf who fell in well ;

This love makes me Ponder in the wet dreams of well ,
Have you ever heard of it? The song of lover for you ;
I am here wrote the whole inch of my blood in the words;
My words died in the saga of your charming face ;
I wished I would die in the vivid dream of your love .
This feelings makes my heart incongruous in your love ;

Lullabies of the Night that spoken in the dream ;
Is simulating in the house of the Peace in Kabbah,
How Pocius the love of the lover, that make home
In the road of the where God house is Kabah ;
I am here in the middle of the sea for looking the
House that borrow that love hearts in the house

Closing my eyes on the curvature of the sigh ,
The dilemma melted me into an illusion.

Oh ! You who hear the silence in the words,
Do you hear the steps of my foot in sadness?
The shallow mind of mine is trapped in the smile of yours,
I am here, lying in the mud in the illusion of yours
Should I catch the dream or drown in a dilemma?
Closing my eyes in the dreams of yours to be mine!

My love “ Is it right to call you mine?” ;
As each night I fell in love with you ;
The days is not mine but the favour of you ;
I can’t think myself beyond you in the world;
My love “Is it right to call you mine?”
Life is wasteland without the sigh of you ;
I give you my heart and my life ;
My love “Is it right to call you mine?”
As I didn’t hear any trace of yours ;
But still wounded my heart in love of you;
My love” Let come to sit beside me”
I look up in your eyes and make my sigh yours forever.

"Oh! Sweetheart" my heart lived
In uttering resemblance of you,

My hands flicked to catch
The memorable touch of you,
"Oh! Sweetheart" the world is
Awful; I want to be with you,
"Oh! Sweetheart" my heart is burning
To trapped in scenario of you,
"Oh!Sweetheart" I wanna beshine
Like the moon in dwell nights for you,
"Oh! Sweetheart" I wanna fall in love
That last in eternity with you,
"Oh! Sweetheart" the death would not
Not gonna be our Place,
It's a delightful time of life!

The tiny drops of rain blurred
The love in each fall of it
The one tiny drop is fall on my lips
It has the splash of upcoming scenario
The love that delivered in the grasp
Of the hush and the bonding of the two loves
Don't close your Eyes in the dark nights
Where Rain Falls and Nobody could could
Able to see us , It would be the time when
Heart dance in the rhythm of the lights

ROYA WAHAB

Oh! Woe to My Innocent heart
That fall in the love of you ;
I am reckless like the sun for you ;
I am darker than night for you ;
I am lonely like the stars for you ;
Oh! Way to My Innocent Heart
That fall in the love of you;
I am Incapable to do anything for you ;
I am reckless like grass in wasteland
Oh! Woe to My Innocent heart
That fall in the love of you;
Darling! Close your eyes , let hold my hands
To walk in the place beyond right and wrong
I found it in the Plane of love with you
Oh! Woe to My Innocent Heart
That fall in the love of you ;
Oh! Woe to My Innocent Heart
That fall in the love of you ;

May , My lord forgive me ;
As it would be My last Breath ;

And the name of you is on my tongue ;
Your love fragile me in the days
To Dreams, the words were not form
But meant to write in the love of you,
May, My lord forgive me,
As it would be the My last breath
And the name of you in my tongue
How difficult is it to write yourself?
In the Plain Paper , Your Presence
Make me Alive , Let me sleep in the
Painful dream of the charming illusion
When It's Vanish don't ask about myself
May , My lord forgive me ;
As it would be My last Breath ;
And the name of you is on my tongue ;
Because You encapsulated me into you!

Your Innocence sooth the hurricane in my Heart
Your arrival brings the shore in the ocean
There is something that you bring
My heart, Had the song for you ;
That didn't stick with you ;
Your Innocence sooth the hurricane in my heart
Your arrival brings the shore in the ocean
You have tangled in the cool breeze of the ocean.

I looked at his eyes and said
" There is something I missed
From the days we meet. I think
It's myself or my feelings which
Emphasis. I don't know how to
Exactly show what is on my heart
Has to reveal for you but there is something
Which I have only for you"
That is uncertain from the desire to have
Something from you, it's not about to
Fell in love with you but it's about
I found love in you. So, " I love you"
It's not just the beautiful but the emotions
Which I hold for you.

The Melody of you stuck me in the new taste of life ;
It has the uncanny voice of the past ;
The melody gives me the new sign of life ;
I love you, I love you, I love you
I swear that day didn't bring the dawn and the
The night didn't hazle the darkness in the sigh of you ;
I love you, I love You, I love You
I swear the melody of you have taste of life
I love the taste of the fire that burn me
In the splashing love of the stranger
The window between us broke the home
Of dreams and I have nothing left beside your lover.

The love knock the dreams of fairy tales

As you step in the corner of it, you have
The aroma of love in the stage of dullness
My heart was devastated and broken in the
In the vast land of sorrow and pain, You are the
A light that came in my life, You have the
The sweetness of tea and the smell of flowers
As my heart gloom in each step for you ;
The love knock the dreams of fairy tales
As you step in the corner of it, you have
In the smooth road of the little Mistake ,
I carved my existence with you in tales
Of life ,It can touch my skin and fell out
The existence of the words into the layers
Of Cage that bonded sweet love ,
remembrance Carry the gesture of the door
that Knock each steps of the love as
Each step kissed by the wind!

You may devour words of hate towards us ;
In the valley of tulips the love blossom in our blood
The cold breeze shimmers the rise of the sun;
In the chest of Asia, the spring brings the new Year,
The words were died and born to hearken ;
Happiness dwells in a vivid wall of Pain ;
We fall and we will be a rise
Bravery reiterates in the heart of "Khorasan"!
Khorasan was the city of the love and the Purity
Of angelic soul , it have the fire of sun and the rise
Of tulips in a bunch of flowers that evolves love.

I couldn't able to abandon yourself from my eyes
It carry the untold story of you , the night has
The sweet taste of you , what you did darling
My heart is wrapped in the fragile rode for you
It never abandoned yourself from my eyes
As Yourself dusk out in my eyelashes,
Whenever I have to lift it to see the world
I have seen you, It laminate the soul of two
Lovers in vast and open road on the love
It felt like you deliquescence in my breath
That's drenched out my soul to be yours

The heaven look down in the scenario
Of the beloved, I catch the bubbles of love
In the boil of pain to bloom the rose of love

Darling! My heart caged in the soul of you
The stars sparkled more under the shadow of your love
It loomed and daazile the smile in the boil of blood
Which I drink each night in the fear to lose you
The heaven are filled with tiny stones of thorns
That stuck in the heart of lovers , I sip
The boil of wine under the moonlight , So
My lover has stayed with me till eternity !
I wish for the love that long last till my last breath
The eyes were rolled up and the hairs stuck together
You tell me your favourite song and I will sing for you that
I wish all your pain will be pain that I decorate myself with !

If someone asked me what is love?
I will tell them love is like frequence of Rose
The first touch of petals and hurts like thorns
Love has the taste of wine that sip by Lovers
If someone asked me what is love?
I will tell them Love is reckless like candles
The first touch burns it till it humid it with wind
Love has the taste of wine that sip by Lovers
If someone asked me what is love?
I will tell them love is like a moon in darkness
Which light dwells in the darkest night for lovers
Love has the taste of wine that sip by Lovers
Love has the taste of wine that sip by Lovers
To drink sip by sip for the taste of the lovers

The autumn breaks the moist drops of rain
I feel you in each part of my body
The song of love sung by birds
And mingled in the threads of love
The autumn breaks the moist drops of rain
I feel you in the sight of my shadow
In each footstep, you came closer
And mingled in the threats of love
My love , you have the fragrance of the
Rose that encapsulates the lover in beauty.
Someday , I wish I be your buyer and you
Decocrate me in each step of your house
It's like the Persian phase stuck in English.

Moon never walk behind the stars ;
Yet the night smuggled the beauty of stars
Oh! My lover the time with you enchanter my heart
I feel you in each corner of my heart
Do you hear the beat? I am not the
One who might entangled the words with
The beauty of her but I am the most
Awful lover that feel in the love of you
The world seems nothing infront of you
My love , My words are never be capable
To tangle the aroma of my heart in it.
My heart, do you listen to the sound of love?
I dishevelled in the love of you, You are the thirst
Of my heart; which I want to drink at midnight
In the shore of the calm sea near the dream of love;
Words born and die to torn the beauty of my love
In the vast Paper of hope beyond dusk and truth

My Hands Longing to hold a hand of Companion
In mid dark night to be the only star to shine
When I feel flatten their words be one's
Whom feel like an only rose in garden
There is no secret Shelter the lovers
So , I will give you my skin to become my soul.
My Hands longing to hold a hand of Companion
In Mid day to be the only rays that stuck on me
When I feel joyful with the aroma of their words
It blooms the story of exuberance

The Glass of Red Wine has taste of soreful Love;
From Hands of lover it enhance the story of Heaven
The crisp and the taste of arrival of the Love ;
Burn the sigh of light in my Heart to dwell the streets
The Lamp has turned into ashes to reach the echo
Of the core of ocean to diverged in aroma of Love
Its unusual to see the love in Plain of the surreal hell
It burns the fire in each step of it .

The echo of Rain in Arrival of you ;
Enchanter my soul in dreams of you ;
The visit of you in the Purity of Mosque ;
With the cup of Alcohol that Impure the
Vision of faith and calm spirituality.
The echo of Rain in Arvail of you;
Enchanter the heart in the lost dreams of you;
Oh! The Lost lover of my heart and dreams
Let dissolve in my heart like soil in mud

One day shall I meet you in the Garden of Rose
Where we will walk together hand by hand
In the beautiful scenario to hook ourselves in Gaze
Of colours that Played in the bottom of our Heart
You never told me how beautiful it is , to stuck
In the love of you , I bend my knees for you and in
This Position with open arms under stars I all
Said , I love You , I love You , I love You!
In this era of love that stuck in our hearts with
Tragedy , Let me Memorise you like the scared
Book that each Part of body be yours and If I buried
Then it turned in the rhythm of pearls that catch you!

4. Romance in the Air

Romance in the Air

My lips touch the warmth of your Lips ;
It dishalving myself in the boil of glass of wine,

Which I had tasted in my dream once to dissolve ,
In the beat that sung by the melody of someone ;
I appreciate the gesture , yet I am unknown from your
Presence , tho it depends on the scars of the Past ;
That's stabilise by the unknown touch of the of lover
The kiss dissolve in the air by the touch of wine ;
No one ever see how the taste of wine look like ;
It inflamed the taste of the life in the cup of wine

Flipping your hand in my breast is the sign of the lover
We share the aroma of the love in the breath of wet water
Flipping my hair in your hands is the etiquettes of the lover
It becoming the ray of the light as you enter in my soul
Slowly slowly my hands are crawling and you Put me down
In the vast land of the water filled with the sweet love of the lover
I kept you down in the sweet love of mine , the ray of sun
Exotic the first splash of the water from the heaven in the rain
Could you hear the breath? That we tangled in the sigh of love

I wish the day is crawled inside my bed to give inflammable love

It would be ferns of joy and the pain , when you with me
My darling , I wonder how's my life with you in this world
I carved the statues of love and Paintings through my hands
To give structure this land of love though the soul of lovers
I am aint Poetess but keep drown my feelings to escalate one word
Of the love in this wasteland to myself who kept in prison of your heart
It would be the last time that the breath is in charged in the vision of you
My darling , I wonder how's my life without you in this world

"Oh! Romeo" my heart lived
In uttering resemblance of you ,
My hands flicked to catch
The memorable touch of you ,
"Oh! Romeo" the world is
Awful , I want to be with you,
"oh!Romeo" my heart is burning
To be trapped in a scenario of you .
"Oh!Romeo" I wanna be shine
Like moon in dwell nights for you ,
" Oh!Romeo" I wanna fall in love
Till the last in eternity with you .
"Oh! Romeo" the death would
Not gonna be our place ,
Thee it's the delight time of life;
"Oh!romeo" my heart fall
And burst into petals for you .

I couldn't able to abandon yourself from my eyes
Yourself dusk in my eyelashes,
Whenever i have lift it up to see the world
I have seen you ,
It felt like you delinquency in my breath
That's drenched out my soul to be yours!

I never knew how could the feelings for
Beloved be so gracious,
Before I had meet you ,
I never knew how could someone face been
In your sight and thoughts,
Before I meet you,
It's felt like sky down to land and what I
Know the moment that I want to be Yours!

His wordings have an essence of beauty,
In which thee sorrow buried into the love,
That escaped my heart in his Palm
Where the love found me in the phase of your life.
The day night didn't longer resemble myself,
It been a bystander of my love towards you,
Where I breathe in the essence of you
In the desire to be yours.

This feeling is gonna be exotic,
Which burning myself from toe to hair,
Where I kept your vision in the depth of my heart
Your eyes said the attering words of my heart .
As each step my foot moving towards you ,
I felt the grasp of his breathe,
It would be the first time
Heaven touched my heart in the sign of his eyes
When yourself diverging into the arms of beloved ones,
You may close of your eyes,
In the breath to him your each arch of yourself.

Dip in the close eyes , I feel the moist
My heart burn to catch the warmth of you,
I curved my hands in the scenario
To dip you inside the heart of mine ;
The nights winds give fast , the life
Sung the wet song of the love

My red lips have the beauty of love
It gashes the strawberry of love
When it wet it gives the wine of love
My red lips have the beauty of love
Drunk in the Midnight it touches the
Thirst of the lovers ;

Some Nights I want someone to be with me ,
In the dark Night to bloom the song of it ,
No haze can touch the shore of mY sight ,
I feel lonely in the Mid Night of the love ,
No one can share the song of Nights ,
It bloom in the ray of light ;
Some Nights in the ray of light;
Some nights I want someone to be with me;

The lips meet to the thirst of it ;
No one can adore the thirst of it ;
It melt and burn together in the scenario of it
The lips meet the strawberry of life ;
I want to touch and lick it ;
It depends on the thirst of the eve;
You can solve the heart but how can dissolve the flame,

Smelling lips of the cherry smash the rose of the love ;
You can hear it twist it and tangled it with the ray of light ;
Smelling lips of the cherry smash the nights of lovers ;
Woe! To my heart who can ever the words of it ;
Smashing lips of the cherry hear the unseen truth of the life ;
I want to die in this truth and live in the lie of this words;
Tho! To my heart whoever hear the sweeten taste of the love ;
Smashing lips of cherry tangled in the love of you ,

In thirsty nights of love , I want your warmth that tangled myself
It amazed the nights of the lover and truth of the myself ;
It gives you the nice comfort and the warmth that delight in vision of the heaven
I give myself in the dilemma of the night that soaked in the arms of the lover
I give you myself in the aroma of the night that heard my breath
It touches you at night , that gives me the aroma of myself.

Night says more than darkness
When the silence graciously

Holding you in your arms
It's just a mirage
Or a dream which I saw
At the first blink of my eyes in morning
Till night when slowly sleep catches my eyes
And it's you whom I'm finding in each corner
No longer heart aches loneliness
When I found you everywhere
I know it's just a mirage or a dream
Or melody which I seek to be mine
Viscously it's not a Poetry or words
It's a sweetest or bitter truth

Isn't anomalous that wind touch us
On grief that touch riddim saga of love
And as the hands move to hold that touch
Isn't anomalous that sigh flattered in haze
That turning in Pieces of the breath
Well we couldn't touch nor see the haze
But yet it riddim in the touch of that wind
Isn't anomalous how the words Pleaded
To tore and frame the magic of love.

Printed by Libri Plureos GmbH in Hamburg,
Germany